T0380785

BLINDING GLIMPSES OF THE OBVIOUS

**Love..Relationships..
Money..Family..Work..
Marriage..Morality..Politics..
Sex..and More...**

Revealing Insights, LOL Humour and Good Old Common Sense.

RAJAN JETLEY

Archway Publishing books may be ordered through booksellers or by contacting:

Archway Publishing
1663 Liberty Drive
Bloomington, IN 47403
www.archwaypublishing.com
844-669-3957

ISBN: 978-1-6657-3086-0 (sc)
ISBN: 978-1-6657-3088-4 (hc)
ISBN: 978-1-6657-3087-7 (e)

Library of Congress Control Number: 2022917838

Print information available on the last page.

Archway Publishing rev. date: 03/21/2023

I dedicate this book to a bottle of good Vodka and my many evenings of solitude and contemplation spent in its wonderful company. The best parties are always for two.

Although there may be little in the way of new thought, there is much in the way of new expression.

INTRODUCTION

What a wonderful and varied life of experiences I have had. Born in India, at seventeen I lived and studied in the United States on an American Field Service exchange scholarship for a year. I lived with a wonderful American family and spent my last year of high school in Chatham, New Jersey. This was in 1967 and 1968. I saw the effect of the Vietnam War on America and witnessed the anti-war movement at its peak. I experienced the shock and horror of the assassinations of Robert Kennedy and Martin Luther King Jr.. Music was from those who are legends now: the Doors, Jimi Hendrix, Bob Dylan, Cohen; even the Monkees were "Groovin'." And then there was Soul Records, which had been established by Berry Gordy in 1964 as part of the Motown Records Corporation. The artists included Aretha Franklin, the Supremes, Sam and Dave, Marvin Gaye, and a host of other legends. The Beatles released *Sgt. Pepper's Lonely Hearts Club Band* and the movie *The Graduate*, which greatly challenged existing social norms and introduced the young Dustin Hoffman, was released.! It was a defining twelve months.

It was a time when if you said you were Indian, people thought you had jumped the reservation! The only things associated with India were Ravi Shankar and the sitar, good incense, and the bleeding Madras Shirt, all thanks to the hippies. For a seventeen-year-old boy from India, it was magic.

I have since lived and traveled in many countries. My career has spanned almost fifty years. I sold various products and services across many geographic locations. From the cities and village bazaars of India to the boardrooms of London, Paris, Singapore, New

York, and most major cities, I sold cigarettes, office equipment, soap and detergents, cookies, hotel rooms, airline seats, chicken wings, and even Companies. I met and knew Presidents and Prime Ministers, the world's most powerful Captains of finance and industry, Gurus and soothsayers, great writers, actors, and musicians. In this long journey from the crowded bazaars of India, selling cigarettes by the packet to retailers on my bicycle, to becoming the youngest CEO of Air India, a major international airline, I had wonderful successes and some disappointing failures.

Each experience is a thread in the fabric of a person's mind. Every human being weaves a fabric of his or her experiences that are as unique as the person's fingerprints. We observe events, interpret them, and express our thoughts and events uniquely. These thoughts often come as flashing insights and glimpses, which we process through the filter of our individual fabric. It may be that the thought or event may not be new, yet there is much space in the way of its new expression.

The wonderful thing about language is in its ability to convey a thought, a feeling, an experience, and almost anything to others. The imaginative user has the freedom to convey his or her thoughts in a hundred different ways. That's the beauty of expression, and the artistry of articulation. It has always fascinated me. The more succinct, the more beautiful!

I am convinced that in the journey of human beings over millions of years, every experience must have been lived somewhere at some time. Every thought has been expressed in one way or another. And as I have said before, even if there is very little in the way of new thought or experience, there is still much in the beauty of the way it is expressed or articulated. This belief is the driving force behind this compilation of thoughts. I have tried to convey in my own words a few revealing insights into our everyday lives. It may help in presenting a new perspective or a new insight on living and understanding everyday life.

If anything in the book should even remotely reek of wisdom, I assure you it's purely unintentional. While I have been compiling these thoughts for the last twenty-odd years,

I took the precaution of publishing them only after I'd turned seventy, hoping that at least some people may take them seriously, if only in deference to my age.

Finally, I struggled with the format of this book. I first thought I would categorize it in obvious chapters: family, work, relationships, and politics, for example. I found that in reality it was hard to compartmentalize these ideas so easily. Every day in life is a mix of these aspects crazily woven together. So I just left it that way. You can open any page and read it in any sequence. It's presented as it came to me, and I wrote it. I recommend you read it the same way. To highlight the uniqueness of each thought they are all presented as differently and crazily as possible.

Each one a BGO!

If contentment be your lifelong goal, look for it in your attitude towards life. You can find it equally in both success and failure.

P1 # Q1

Exiting a market bubble is like having unprotected sex. It's very hard to pull out at the right time even though you know there is a risky outcome just ahead.

P1 # Q2

With every act of caring, you take for granted, you untie a knot that holds the relationship together.

P1 # Q3

You demean your wealth when
you bargain with a poor man.

P2 # Q4

The secret to success may be always
putting yourself first. The secret to
happiness is exactly the opposite.

P2 # Q5

Pride is the most difficult bridge to cross in the mending of a broken relationship.

P2 # Q6

If you wish to avoid constant disappointment in life, learn to live with lower expectations.

P2 # Q7

The joys that wealth and power promise to bring into our lives may in reality be vastly exaggerated.

P3 # Q8

Far worse than being born into poverty is descending into it.

P3 # Q9

Beware that you are most vulnerable to a foolish and emotional over reaction when your vanity is hurt.

P3 # Q10

An unrealistic expectation of perfection in each other lies at the heart of many of our broken relationships.

P4 # Q11

It's a strange paradox of morality when the most corrupt among us show zero tolerance for the dishonesty of others.

P4 # Q12

Every turning point in life that is unexpected only serves to enhance our belief in the role of destiny in our lives.

P4 # Q13

The ability to recognize
a great idea is as great
a talent as the ability to
generate one.

P5 # Q14

**A risk is not a risk if its
worst consequences are
acceptable.**

P5 # Q15

**Your deepest secrets are
held by the ones you trust
the most. Their vulnerability
is your weakest point.**

P5 # Q16

P7 # Q17

Resist the temptation to look too closely at anything you really admire, unless you are committed to finding its imperfections.

P7 # Q17

Unlike friendship, love is mostly a fading emotion. Its best chance of survival is always amongst friends.

P7 # Q18

Winning or losing should only be about the game. Sadly it always turns personal.

P7 # Q19

Very often success or failure in our lives is owed to the effect of a single relationship.

P8 # Q20

The Third World is well defined as a place where every functionary of the State considers himself an equal and rightful partner in the upside of any business he happens to deal with requiring his approval.

P8 # Q21

There is no better display of national character than the road manners of its citizens.

P8 # Q22

Presenting people with choices instead of solutions reduces conflict, improves acceptance, and ensures adherence.

P8 # Q23

Whenever you like someone instantly, notice he or she often looks familiar.

P10 # Q24

The surest guarantee of loyalty to a leader is the leader's ability to make every individual team member feel that he or she has a special relationship with the leader.

P10 # Q25

Influence is an even more potent force than authority.

P10 # Q26

Work is a means to an end when you have nothing. When you achieve the end, work becomes a means to preserving your achievement. We labor on.

P11 # Q27

Very often the secret to accumulating a fortune lies in making tiny gains repeatedly, instead of risking everything on a single great gamble.

P11 # Q28

The measure of our loyalty to anyone should never be based on our support of them in an unjust cause.

P11 # Q29

There is nothing more exhausting than a repeated thought.

P13 # Q30

The longevity of a relationship rests not only on the appreciation of each other's strengths, but also on the tolerance of each other's weaknesses.

P13 # Q31

In order to succeed, keep your objective clear, and your strategy flexible.

P13 # Q32

Success is not just about the use of your strengths. It's equally about the control of your weaknesses.

P13 # Q33

The only place on earth where the Lord hears no prayers is the golf course.

P14 # Q34

Power may flow from the position you hold. It also flows from your relationship with the powerful.

P14 # Q35

A shocking turning point in attitude comes when you realize you have fewer days ahead of you than behind you.

P14 # Q36

There is no better measure of your maturity than your level of tolerance.

P16 # Q37

The challenge of an effective peacemaker lies on one factor alone: the level of trust the person enjoys on both sides.

P16 # Q38

Life's troubles seem to strike suddenly, like lightning. In reality, we fail to listen carefully to the rumbling and distant thunder that almost always precedes a storm.

P16 # Q39

There is nothing greater than a single thought to give the sweetest pleasure or inflict the severest pain.

P17 # Q40

Don't admire too greatly the qualities of anyone you worship or idolize. You may find a mere human hiding inside.

P17 # Q41

Pulling rank is the most popular and least effective style of management.

P17 # Q42

Sensitivity is ironically our best and worst quality.

P17 # Q43

Learning from experience is as safe as asking a guy who just crossed a mine field for directions.

P18 # Q44

Sex is merely an act that is used equally for the bodily gratification of lust and the soulful expression of love.

P18 # Q45

Never be afraid to change your mind. You always know more today than you knew yesterday.

P18 # Q46

At first, we seek success to achieve wealth and prominence and then long for anonymity to enjoy the same.

P18 # Q47

Your children will imbibe your weaknesses effortlessly while you struggle endlessly to pass your strengths on to them.

P19 # Q48

The challenges of bringing up children in an affluent home are far greater than in an impoverished one.

P19 # Q49

Wealth can create some amazing illusions: youthfulness in the elderly and wisdom in the young.

P19 # Q50

The head is conditioned by conventional learning, and the heart is led by natural instinct.

P20 # Q51

The claim of pedigree in modern times requires only a single generation of wealth or power.

P20 # Q52

We conveniently credit every success to our work and ability and blame every failure on either luck or the will of God.

P20 # Q53

Every generation has the obligation to protect the future of the next generation, just as the next generation has the duty of preserving the legacy of the present one.

P21 # Q54

There is no better investment in life than in a sound and long term relationship.

P21 # Q55

A fundamental difference between Western and Eastern cultural approaches toward bringing up children is that the West encourages independence and the East interdependence. Each may envy the other.

P21 # Q56

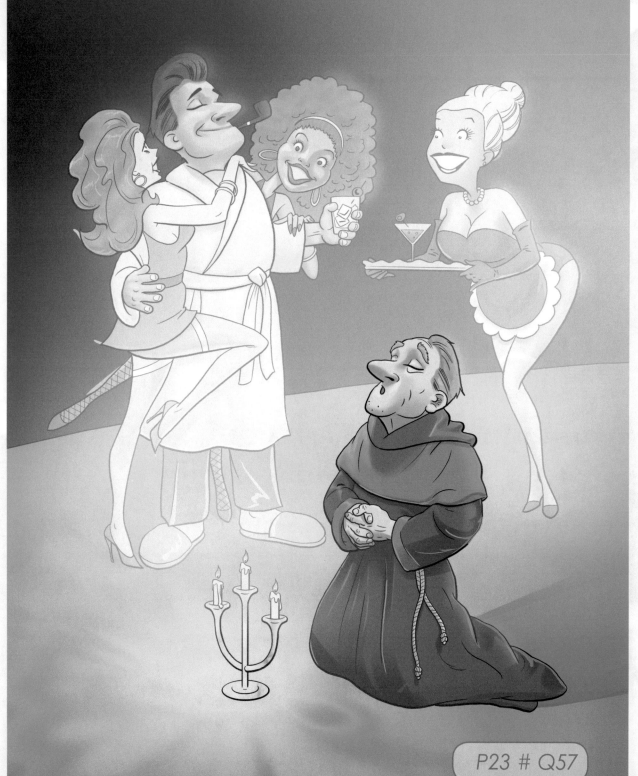

P23 # Q57

As sexual prowess begins
to descend, religious
fervor begins to ascend.

P23 # Q57

There is a world of difference
between spending money on the
things you need and the things you
want. The first is a requirement
and the second an indulgence.

P23 # Q58

The difference between the pleasure of
spending money you earn and the money
you inherit is the same as in the taste of
the fruit you grow and the fruit you buy.

P23 # Q59

Does every lost
opportunity not seem the
greatest one you ever had?

P24 # Q60

**The cost of doing business with
a friend is mostly paid by the
friendship itself.**

P24 # Q61

Belligerence is a sure giveaway
of the weaker cause.

P24 # Q62

There is no greater hurt in a
relationship than a realization of
being used.

P24 # Q63

P24 # Q60

The ability of a single human being, to produce more food than they can consume, allows for all the other great achievements of humanity.

P26 # Q64

Your children will always treat you as they see you treat their grandparents.

P26 # Q65

As it is with all things in nature, most relationships sadly, deteriorate with time.

P26 # Q66

You may have found contentment in life if all you want in the future is for the present to continue.

P28 # Q67

The cost of destroying a competitor is almost always more than the premium you pay to buy him out.

P28 # Q68

The ability to compartmentalize your relationships successfully is the key to a wide sphere of trust and acceptability.

P28 # Q69

No political party can make more
of a difference than the other in
the fortunes of the common people
when, in spite of political change,
the bureaucracy which deals with the
people remains the same.

P29 # Q70

Why do we feel things may go wrong
if we stop worrying about them?

P29 # Q71

The soundest foundation of all
good legislation lies in leaving
no room for more than a single
interpretation.

P29 # Q72

The conflict between what
we want to do and what we
have to do is the difference
between desire and duty.

P30 # Q73

Nothing will be as important
tomorrow as it may seem today.

P30 # Q74

The best celebrations in life are often best enjoyed just by two!

P30 # Q75

Unutilized Capital will eventually diminish in value unless it rejuvenates itself through the flow of fresh blood of returns on new investments.

P31 # Q76

Perseverance more than the power of argument can often help in wearing the opposition down.

P31 # Q77

Businesses can only be created by a spirit of risk and instinct. They cannot, however, survive and prosper without professionalism and prudence.

P31 # Q78

Every uproar over a triviality must be recognized as a ploy for attention.

P33 # Q79

The survival and longevity of all advisors depends on their ability to underplay the fact that the boss's great ideas ever came from them.

P33 # Q80

Neutrality is a risky choice. In times of trouble, you have no friends.

P33 # Q81

Dependence is the strongest bond of all.

P34 # Q82

Never underestimate the contribution of your wealth and position to your charm and popularity.

P34 # Q83

Gratitude is the most powerful of all obligations.

P34 # Q84

Ego blurs the objective.

P34 # Q85

P34 # Q82

The bonds of a relationship built on pursuit and perseverance are often weak and temporary.

P36 # Q86

What is charitably described as a midlife crisis is in truth a shocking realization of creeping impotence.

P36 # Q87

There is absolutely no future in living in the past.

P36 # Q88

Although miracles defy logic, they also provide a perfectly logical explanation for all blind faith.

P37 # Q89

You cannot expect your children to be like you if you gave them everything you never had.

P37 # Q90

Your reaction to any act must be based on your judgement of its intent and not on the act alone.

P37 # Q91

In many ways a fool's paradise guarantees a happier life.

P37 # Q92

As a leader, the aggressive and the incompetent will often seek your attention. Always remember to also seek out the quiet and competent.

P38 # Q93

Patience is a virtue created for all matters whose quick resolution is actually beyond our control.

P38 # Q94

It's no surprise that we live under the wonderful illusion that we have a lot of time. Without this and plans for the future, life would be hard to live.

P38 # Q95

Regret may be a healing balm for our own soul, but it rarely heals the wounds inflicted.

P39 # Q96

It is hypocritical to merely recognize a person's special qualities and achievements and not reward them materially.

P39 # Q97

The wealthy crave relevance as much as the relevant seek wealth.

P39 # Q98

Attraction may be momentary. Beauty is timeless.

P39 # Q99

Remember to grow up along with your children.

P39 # Q100

An abundant inheritance
seldom leads to the creation
of a greater fortune.

P40 # Q101

Great wealth is best nurtured
with middle-class values.

P40 # Q102

Making it in life has one wonderful
advantage: you don't need to be on
your best behavior at all times.

P40 # Q103

If religion was not a business of vested
interests promoting different faiths,
there may be peace on earth.

P40 # Q104

P40 # Q101

Religion is not an essential
part of spirituality.

P42 # Q105

Forgiveness is rarely more
than a practical solution.

P42 # Q106

The instinct to win constantly must
be based on our primal need to
survive. It is destructive to bring it
to every situation in modern life.

P42 # Q107

**Divorce is rarely about not wanting to be together.
It is mostly about not being able to be together.**

P42 # Q108

There are three important stages in a parent-child relationship: proactive in infancy to protect them, interactive in youth to mentor them, and judgmental in maturity to lose them

P43 # Q109

The argument over whose is the true God lies at the heart of all religious conflict, till you ask the question: can there really be more than one?

P43 # Q110

Faith is the balm applied to soothe the insecurity of uncertainty.

P43 # Q111

Once you truly accept the existence of just one God, you cease to see the dividing lines between religions.

P44 # Q112

Irrelevance is the first step toward loneliness and a major cause of it.

P44 # Q113

Fidelity is conveniently about high expectations of your partner but seldom of yourself.

P44 # Q114

The quickest path to someone's marital bed is often by first winning the trust of the spouse.

P45 # Q115

Consensus only guarantees a team's commitment. It's not a substitute for great leadership, which assures success.

P45 # Q116

The most important quality in a nation's leader is the ability to create a national consensus.

P45 # Q117

We make the same mistakes repeatedly and never learn from them. Even a bad experience has very little effect over our basic nature.

P45 # Q118

A person's most attractive attributes for the opposite sex may fleetingly lie in the attractiveness of their bodies. They lastingly however lie in the qualities between their ears and in the thickness of their wallets!

P46 # Q119

failure and stories of unfulfilled love are romanticized best and are the substance of great Classics. feel-good stories are only meant for children and rarely remembered.

P46 # Q120

Wealth begets indulgences.
Poverty has no time for frivolity.
It has survival to attend to.

P46 # Q121

Dependence that binds provokes
hatred and resentment.
Dependence that empowers begets
loyalty and admiration.

P48 # Q122

A cynical definition of the relationship between an old beast and a young beauty is that he has the means and she wants his early end.

P48 # Q123

Arbitrage is often the refuge of the unsure.

P48 # Q124

**Everything at its zenith is by definition
at the beginning of its decline.**

P48 # Q125

Be aware that the thinnest line may divide the space between helping and smothering someone you love.

P49 # Q126

You may start to live when you accept the fact that you are not going to live forever.

P49 # Q127

Be aware that the greatest power to influence you often lies with people who lead you to believe they need nothing from you.

P49 # Q128

Popularity is often
lonely, but never alone.

P50 # Q129

The legacy of colonization often persists in the relationship between people and their governments. The colonizer nations continue to be served by their governments, and the once colonized nations continue the tradition of serving their government masters.

P50 # Q130

The most disarming thing in endearing yourself to someone is making them believe that you are dependent on them but not a burden.

P50 # Q131

P50 # Q129

When you look back on your success in life, you may recall a door that was opened and that one opportunity that someone gave to you. Remember to do that for someone as well.

P52 # Q132

The need to know each other well in any relationship must stop at the point of intrusiveness.

P52 # Q133

There is no greater power to disarm the opponent than a show of absolute confidence.

P52 # Q134

Don't weaken the bonds of a close relationship by an intense scrutiny of its every interaction. The closest ones allow for the most space.

P53 # Q135

In a political re-election, remember you first fight your past performance and then your current opponent.

P53 # Q136

Living a lie every day is a most torturous and exhausting burden.

P53 # Q137

Your ultimate relationship obsessions
are focused on only two people: the
one that you love the most and the
one that you hate the most. Often,
they may be the same person.

P54 # Q138

You can sometimes buy people.
You can rarely own them.

P54 # Q139

The thought of a life beyond
death often helps to make
living more bearable today.

P54 # Q140

**Only fools gamble with their money
if they already have enough of it.**

P54 # Q141

Remember someone can only control you if you care about the consequences of upsetting that person.

When it comes to love, no other fine human quality gets a chance to show its beauty until physical attraction first opens the door.

Emotional compatibility is the longest lasting bond in any relationship. It survives long after many other binding ties have faded.

The money and power of a politician seldom lies in his own bank account. It lies in the influence he has over the coffers of the national treasury and the wealth of his supporters.

P56 # Q145

Often the ability to do you harm gives someone a greater power than his or her ability to do you good.

P56 # Q146

Regret but never mourn a loss unless you have lost the will to fight and win again.

P56 # Q147

Give forgiveness as sincerely as you would ask for it.

P56 # Q148

Is there ever true forgiveness or is there mostly a realistic compromise?

P57 # Q149

The lure to risk infidelity only strikes when you feel completely trusted.

P57 # Q150

Competence, perseverance and relationship management are the three great pillars of success.

P57 # Q151

A day's consideration is often the difference between a quick and a wise decision.

P57 # Q152

P59 # Q153

Only a petty person would put on airs of self importance, when asked for something really small.

P59 # Q153

An uncontrollable addiction is the ultimate love-hate relationship.

P59 # Q154

As critical as the world may be when you are alive, it is ironically charitable once you are dead.

P59 # Q155

The maturity of old age helps lift the curse of false pride.

P59 # Q156

Failure is often competence
denied an opportunity.

P60 # Q157

**A short memory is often the
secret to long-lasting happiness.**

P60 # Q158

A mentor enables. A patron
merely provides.

P60 # Q159

**Power and wealth, when
separated, are longing lovers.**

P60 # Q160

Disciples once sought out great gurus.
Gurus now seek out great disciples.

P60 # Q161

P60 # Q157

Prayer is the currency you use to build your spiritual bank balance.

P62 # Q162

Success is also about listening carefully. You never know when something you hear presents an unexpected opportunity.

P62 # Q163

Rationality is the first virtue to disappear in the newly love-struck.

P62 # Q164

The pleasure of being in a good relationship can only be compared with the relief of getting out of a bad one.

P62 # Q165

Sadly the shadow cast by the smallest scandal in our lives looms larger than the bright lights of our many achievements.

P63 # Q166

Suspicion slowly burns the soul.

P63 # Q167

Morality is an acquired standard. In nature there is only basic instinct.

P63 # Q168

The ultimate orgasm following both wealth and power is public adulation.

P63 # Q169

Ignorance rather than intent is often the cause of many a destructive act. It deserves forgiveness and understanding.

P65 # Q170

The best is always in the past only because the future hasn't arrived yet.

P65 # Q171

Beneath the insatiable appetite of every great philanderer is the absence of a truly loving relationship.

P65 # Q172

A democracy with compromised institutions is only a dictatorship in disguise.

P65 # Q173

Our every act of charity
first heals ourselves.

P66 # Q174

Eventually a storm must follow the calm.

P66 # Q175

Hope and endeavor march
hand in hand to achieve
success. If one falters, the
journey ends.

P66 # Q176

A true leader has the ability to treat
some poor performance patches by
his team merely as periods of learning.

P66 # Q177

Marriage is a binding contract signed to protect the relationship from a fading emotion called love.

P68 # Q178

The inevitable end to an illicit affair is almost always a tear over the cheek and a check in the pocket.

P68 # Q179

When forgiveness is the only practical option, we find a logical reason.

P68 # Q180

Shyness and insecurity are often opposite sides of the same coin.

P68 # Q181

P68 # Q178

Contentment also means needing only what your means can provide and accepting only what your relationships can give.

P70 # Q182

Interdependence and common purpose are stronger family bonds than common ancestry.

P70 # Q183

Faith in destiny strengthens when you realize that many pursuits unfulfilled in life may have led you away from the edge of a hidden precipice and to a better outcome.

P70 # Q184

Wealth with anonymity is the
goal of the truly evolved.

P71 # Q185

A person at peace with his or her conscience stands unaffected by criticism.

P71 # Q186

Few of us would choose predictability
over some uncertainty in life.

P71 # Q187

Civilization requires us to live by the common rules of society. This avoids the chaos that would follow if each of us followed our natural instincts.

P71 # Q188

The work environment is often more important in job performance than the monetary remuneration.

P72 # Q189

Those who wield power tend to avoid a public display of a close relationship with their colleagues. Somewhere deep inside is a fear not only of shifting the limelight momentarily but also empowering the person unintentionally.

P72 # Q190

No one wants anyone who no one else wants. Everyone wants those who everyone else wants. We instinctively follow the herd.

P72 # Q191

If we all learned only from the experience of those gone before us without ever experimenting on our own, most progress and innovation would cease.

P73 # Q192

Every lawyer owes his or her existence to two versions of the same story.

P73 # Q193

The resolution of many conflicts between States is often based, not on the merits of the cause, but on the personal equation of the leadership on both sides.

P73 # Q194

The reason for your casino addiction may be the memory of a single win.

P73 # Q195

There is something about
wealth and power that
breeds an instinctive
distrust of others.

P74 # Q196

Nature did not necessarily
build the strength of our bonds
of love and blood equally.

P74 # Q197

No legal obligation is
ever strong enough,
to force an unwilling
relationship into a
true partnership.

P74 # Q198

No parent ever succeeded in forcing a close relationship between unwilling siblings.

P75 # Q199

The irony of politically convenient but ideologically differing coalitions especially when pandering to minor parties, is that they make a mockery of the democratic principle that the will of the majority must prevail.

P75 # Q200

The doors to any relationship can be opened first by finding a single common interest.

P75 # Q201

In punishing a loved one, you can stop your support of the person but never your concern.

P76 # Q202

A lie told, but not in personal interest, may need to be reevaluated based on its true intent.

P76 # Q203

The extent of abhorrent crime shown in the sensational media is so frequent today that these abominations begin to convey the false and damaging impression of normality.

P76 # Q204

Alcohol abuse blurs the lines between loving and abusive behavior. It hurts the victim and perpetrator equally.

P77 # Q205

Loneliness is the widest spread and best kept secret disease of the human race.

P77 # Q206

The obligation of family ties often prevents us from distributing our wealth to more deserving causes. Blessed are those who have the strength to rise above such bondage.

P77 # Q207

A lasting relationship is built upon transparently sharing our strengths and vulnerabilities. This helps hold the relationship together long after the masks of pretense have disappeared.

P78 # Q208

Being a knowledgeable connoisseur of fine wines while being clueless of their real qualities comes easily. Buy the most expensive bottle in the shop.

P78 # Q209

There is no worse enemy in life than one with a deep pocket and a long memory.

P78 # Q210

Procreation is the basic instinct that lies at the heart of all romantic love.

P78 # Q211

P78 # Q208

An empty rice bowl often leads to a greater hunger for religion and spirituality.

P80 # Q212

Never underestimate the sexual attractiveness of a charming conversationalist.

P80 # Q213

Happy people seldom look for a meaning in life. They just live life.

P80 # Q214

Past enemies turned friends do not only carry the burden of proving their loyalty on their shoulders. They must also wear it on their sleeves at all times.

P80 # Q215

A drink is not just a drink. It's a revelation of your hidden talent, strengths, and potential. It shows you who you truly are and can be. It also reveals to others what you really are and who you pretend to be!

P81 # Q216

The strength of the rule of law is in the freedom to rule against the ruler.

P81 # Q217

The definition of being truly wealthy is not only having enough wealth to afford anything you want but also limiting what you want, to what you can afford.

P81 # Q218

A military coup must be the greatest betrayal of a democracy. The guardians of democracy end up enslaving it.

P82 # Q219

Unstinting support makes the strong even stronger. It also makes the weak weaker.

P82 # Q220

Almost all practical problems in life are resolved by writing a large enough check.

P82 # Q221

The task of climbing the corporate ladder includes not just hard work and performance but also the art of taking credit for your and everyone else's work.

P83 # Q222

Old age is defined as a point in our lives, when the kill is even more exhausting than the chase.

P83 # Q223

Every musical instrument invented by man no matter how melodious it be, is merely an accompaniment to the beauty of the human voice and never a substitute for it.

P83 # Q224

When you set the highest
standards of integrity for others,
you also run the risk of the
closest scrutiny for yourself.

P84 # Q225

**Ironically the most honest often fall
prey to the smallest temptation.**

P84 # Q226

Insurgents are seldom defeated by
the State. Often, they are defeated
by the very people they pretend
to defend when they exploit
them on the excuse of seeking
resources to support their cause.

P84 # Q227

A relationship that lacks expectations and requires no maintenance is dead.

P85 # Q228

Marriage may be in conflict with natural instinct, but is essential for the stability of society.

P85 # Q229

There is no greater luxury or blessing than not to be accountable for your time to anyone.

P85 # Q230

When you empower a person of small means with total control over vast resources, temptation is inevitable.

P85 # Q231

You have little right to judge anyone unless you pay their bills.

P86 # Q232

Both the expectation and pursuit of perfection will inevitably end in disillusionment and pain.

P86 # Q233

You only begin to feel old when your parents die.

P86 # Q234

Time changes the relevance and importance of most things in life, that we once held so dear.

P86 # Q235

P86 # Q235

Middle-class values are the best protection against the temptations that wealth and fame bring.

P88 # Q236

Populism eventually impoverishes the very people it is supposed to benefit.

P88 # Q237

Other than a repeated thought, the most exhausting task in the world is keeping a one-year-old-child entertained!

P88 # Q238

Change comes easier and sustains when it is motivated by the incentive of gain rather than forced by the threat of pain.

P88 # Q239

God leaves us with at
least one nagging pain
lest we forget Him in our
otherwise perfect lives.

P90 # Q240

The slide downhill in the career of the great movie stars begins when they begin to play themselves instead of the role they are cast in.

P90 # Q241

There are no perfect Saints, in the world only those who escaped the detection of their flaws.

P90 # Q242

Accountability is a constant and heavy burden.

P91 # Q243

Show me a married couple who didn't vow to stay together only till their children grew up.

P91 # Q244

As you climb the ladder of success, life forces you to recognize people because of who they are. You only begin to recognize people for what they truly are on your way down.

P91 # Q245

The moral burden of carrying
the complete trust of someone,
forces you to take more than
the full responsibility for the
task entrusted to you.

P92 # Q246

The surest way to break up your
marriage is to spend too much
time together.

P92 # Q247

Not everyone who enjoys the pleasure of their own company, is a loner.

P93 # Q248

Don't waste your time giving up all its pleasures for a little longer life. Once you are dead you won't miss the extra time.

P93 # Q249